STORYBOOK

THE DAFFY DUCK

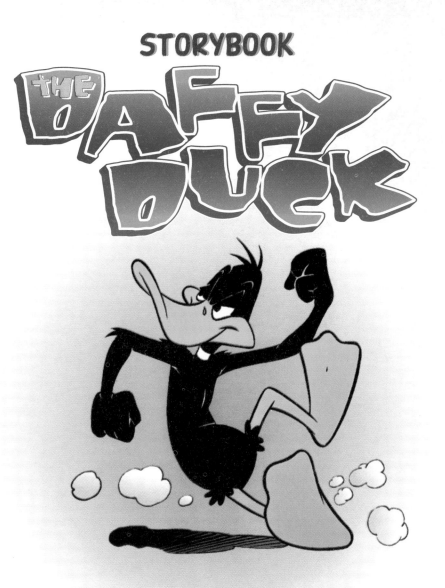

by Julie McNally and Tim Cahill

Illustrated by Sol Studios, Argentina and Landoll, Inc.

It was a beautiful day as Porky Pig drove his old car out to Lake Whatakick. "B-b-boy, a whole w-weekend of c-ca-camping and hunting. I can hardly w-w-wait."

Porky arrived at a clearing and chose the perfect spot to make camp. "After I p-p-pitch my tent, I think I'll g-g-go hunting," Porky said as he unpacked his gear.

Daffy Duck, who was sunning himself nearby, peeked through the bushes and saw Porky about to set his tent. "Show time!" Daffy said, throwing himself between the stake and the ground.

"Hey!" exclaimed Porky. "M-move, you pesky little d-du-d-duck, or I'll c-ca-cook you for d-dinner!"

Porky was furious. "That d-does it!" he cried as he lunged at Daffy. The duck pulled up a huge wooden sign that read: "DUCK SEASON CLOSED. $500 FINE FOR EVEN *TOUCHING* A DUCK!"

"Get the hint, chubby?" Daffy asked.

"Aw, n-nuts, I'm g-g-going fishing," Porky said, picking up his fishing pole and heading for the lake.

"Fishing? Don't mind if I do!" Daffy chuckled to himself as he tiptoed behind Porky to the water's edge.

Porky slowly paddled his canoe out to the middle of the lake. "That duck is c-c-cra-c-c-cra-er, nuts!" Porky said. "I'm g-glad I got away from him." Suddenly, he felt a nibble on the end of his line and started to reel it in!

"Oh, b-boy! It's going to be fish tonight!"
"Hey, can't a duck swim in peace?" a voice said.
It was Daffy, dangling on the end of Porky's line.

Daffy hopped into the boat. "Did you forget already?" he asked him quietly.

"Forget what?" Porky whispered back.

Daffy leaned up to Porky's ear. "NO HUNTING!"

Porky jumped back. "I w-w-wasn't hunting. I was f-f-fishing."

"Same thing to a fish," Daffy said.

Daffy dove off Porky's canoe so forcefully that it sent Porky into the chilly lake.

"Taking a bath?" Daffy asked. "It's not even Saturday night!" He honked Porky's nose. "Woo-hoo! Woo-hoo! Woo-hoo!" screamed the wacky duck as he bounced along the surface of the lake.

When Porky got back to camp, he was shocked to find that crazy duck fixing himself a huge sandwich from Porky's food. "Say, angel-puss—got any ketchup?"

"Th-th-that d-does it!" Porky yelled.

"I can't t-t-take it anymore!" He brought a big pot, grabbed Daffy, stuffed him into it, and set it on the campfire.

"Not so fast, buster," Daffy said. He pointed to a sign on a nearby tree: "DUCK SEASON IS OPEN!"

Porky could hardly believe his eyes.

Daffy could hardly believe *his* eyes, either. He ran quickly behind another sign which read "GO AHEAD, CATCH ALL THE DUCKS YOU WANT—AND DON'T FORGET *THIS* ONE!" Daffy gulped.

Daffy ran for the hills, with Porky hot on his tail
feathers, holding a bag and swinging away with a mallet.
WHOOSH! went the mallet. WHOOSH! WHOOSH!

Daffy was so swift of foot that he dodged, jumped, and ducked every one of Porky's swings. Now, this was good for Daffy, but NOT good for this book . . .

"Ladies and Gentlemen," Daffy announced. "Due to circumstances beyond my control, we are unable to continue this book. But don't worry, I'll tell you how it came out."

"Well, I keep running, running. The little butterball has me on the ropes. He moves in, and everyone figures me for a dead duck."

"But I launch a counter-attack! I shower him with lefts and rights. I'm moving in for the coupy-de-grassy! Then . . ."

"If there are any ladies or children reading, please cover your eyes and ears. Thank you."

"I c-came here to do some hunting, b-b-but I think from now on, I'm j-just gonna c-co-collect stamps!" Porky said.

"Why not?" Daffy said, delirious. "I've started collecting a lovely set of lumps!